3 4028 07605 9238
HARRIS COUNTY PUBLIC LIBRARY

J 306 85 Can
Canet
When   P9-EIE-781
DISCARD $8.99
ocn460712332
1st ed.   11/16/2010

When Times Are Tough

Yanitzia Canetti

Ilustrated by
Romont Willy

Translated by
Alison Keating

© 2009 Yanitzia Canetti
© 2009 Cambridge BrickHouse, Inc.
English translation © 2009 Cambridge BrickHouse, Inc.
All rights reserved. For more information about permission to reproduce selections from
this book, write to Permissions at Cambridge BrickHouse, Inc.
www.BrickHouseEducation.com

Managing Editor: Priscilla Colón
Editors: David Mallick, Heidie Gutierrez
Illustrator: Romont Willy
Designer: Ricardo Potes

Published in the United States by BrickHouse Education.
BrickHouse Education is a division of Cambridge BrickHouse, Inc.

Cambridge BrickHouse, Inc.
60 Island Street
Lawrence, MA 01840
U.S.A.

No part of this book may be reproduced or utilized in any form or by any means,
electronic or mechanical, including photocopying, recording, or by any information
storage and retrieval system without permission in writing from the publisher.

Library of Congress Cataloging-in-Publication Data

Canetti, Yanitzia, 1967-
  When times are tough / Yanitzia Canetti ; illustrated by Romont Willy. -- 1st ed.
    p. cm.
  ISBN 978-1-59835-103-3 (alk. paper)
  1. Families--Economic aspects--Juvenile literature. 2. Unemployed--Juvenile literature.
  3. Thriftiness--Juvenile literature. I. Willy, Romont. II. Title.

HQ744.C36 2009
306.85086'942--dc22

                                                                    2009044993

First Edition
Printed in Singapore
10 9 8 7 6 5 4 3 2 1

A lot of things could change in my life.
My family says that these are tough times.

When times are tough, we might not be able to play video games or watch TV every day.

"We have to save energy," says Mom.

But we can read good books and
make up new games. It will be fun!

When times are tough, we might not be able to go out to eat every weekend.

"We have to spend less," says Dad.

We can make a yummy dinner together in the comfort of our own home. Delicious!

When times are tough, we might not always be able to buy new clothes.

"We already have plenty," says Mom.

But we can give away the clothes we don't use anymore.
We can take better care of the ones we have. We can
even decorate our clothes to give them a cool new look!

When times are tough, Dad might stop working at the furniture shop.

"Don't worry. Dad can do all kinds of things," says Mom.

Dad can work at home. He can repair the neighbors' furniture. He can fix my broken chair. He can plan his own new projects. And he can spend more time with us!

When times are tough, we might not be able to have as many toys.

"You have a lot!" says Dad.

40%

TOYS

But we can give away the toys we don't use. We can create our own toys, too. And we can make toys for other kids!

When times are tough, we might not be able to go away on vacation.

"We'll get to know our own city better," says Mom.

We can make a list of fun things to do. We can visit the city's museums, go for walks in the park, discover new places in our library books, and play with other kids in the neighborhood!

When times are tough, we might not be able to go to ballet or karate class.

"We'll try new activities," says Dad.

But we can go to free community events. We can start our own teams and classes. We can teach other kids what we learned in ballet and karate.

When times are tough, we might not be able to go to summer camp.

"Let's explore as a family!" says Mom.

We can go on nature walks, collect the interesting things we find, go fishing in the river, have a picnic in the park, and even watch the sunset together!

When times are tough, we might not be able to have a clown or magician at my birthday party.

"We can put on our own show!" says Dad.

We can make up new magic tricks.
We can put on funny plays and tell
family jokes. We can improvise!

When times are tough, we might not be able to go everywhere by car.

"It's time to exercise!" says Mom.

We can walk to the corner store and ride our bikes to visit neighbors. It will be great to be outdoors, spend time as a family, and stay healthy.

When times are tough, we might have to sell things that we don't use often.

"Don't you think that we have too much stuff?" asks Dad.

But we can pick out what is most useful. That way, we will have more space to play. We can have fun redecorating the house. And we can easily find the things we lose!

When times are tough, we might have a lot of questions.

"Ask anything you want; we're your family," says Dad.

We can share what we think and offer
ideas to solve problems. We can all
help around the house. And we can
get to know each other better!

When times are tough, Mom and Dad might be worried sometimes.

"The most important thing is that we're together," says Mom.

My sister and I can find fun ways
to make Mom and Dad smile.

When times are tough, we might have to move away from Sunflower Lane.

"We'll have another home of our own one day," say Mom and Dad.

But we can live for a while at our grandparents' or aunt and uncle's house. Grandpa can tell us jokes. Grandma can make us tasty food. And we can play with our cousins every day!

Harris County Public Library
Houston, Texas

Yes, my family is right.
These are tough times.
But we know we will get through them.
Being together makes it easier.

"After the storm,
the sun shines again,"
says Grandma Felicity.